THE GIFT OF LIFE

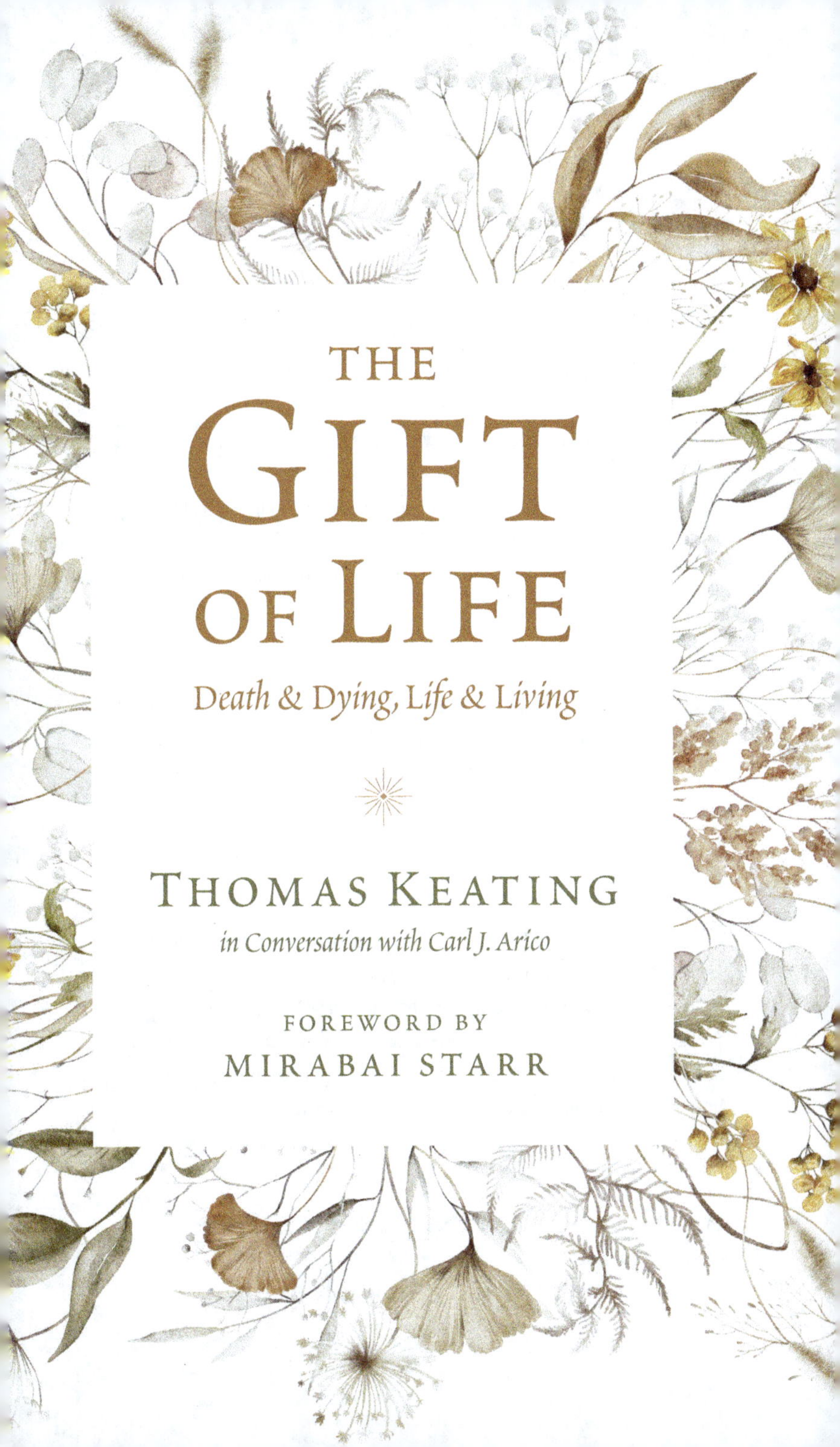

THE GIFT OF LIFE

Death & Dying, Life & Living

✳

THOMAS KEATING

in Conversation with Carl J. Arico

FOREWORD BY
MIRABAI STARR

WAYFARER BOOKS
SAN JUAN MOUNTAINS, COLORADO

First Edition Published in 2026 by Wayfarer Books
Cover Design and Interior Design by Connor Wolfe
TRADE PAPERBACK 978-1-965320-77-8

10 9 8 7 6 5 4 3 2 1

WHOLESALE INQUIRIES? You can find our books available via Ingram, offered with standard trade terms and lifetime returnability. With printing bases in the US, the EU, the UK, and Australia, Wayfarer has the capability to fulfill orders globally. Our titles are available wherever books are sold in paperback, ebook, and audiobook. Find our books at local Indies, Bookshop.org, iTunes, Barnes & Noble, Amazon > US & International, or direct at wayfarerbookstore.com.

WAYFARERBOOKS.ORG
WAYFARERMAGAZINE.COM
WAYFARERBOOKSTORE.COM

TABLE OF CONTENTS

FOREWORD

by Mirabai Starr

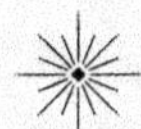

In late October, 2018, I was in Louisville, Kentucky, participating in an interspiritual gathering at an ashram there.

My hosts graciously offered to drive me to Gethsemani Abbey so that I could pay my respects to mystic, peace activist, and interfaith pioneer Thomas Merton, whose work had had a profound influence on me. The night before we were scheduled to make our pilgrimage, another great contemplative who was a personal mentor of mine, Thomas Keating, died. I arrived at the abbey with my heart both broken and full. As I sat in the chapel that afternoon, a prayer rose spontaneously inside me and flowed into the space around me.

"Dear Thomas," I silently called to Merton, "Please gather the soul of Thomas Keating into your arms and carry him to God." My eyes filled with tears as I imagined the two Thomases enfolded in supernatural friendship.

This would seem to be an unsurprising imaginative experience, based on the synchronicity of my arrival at Gethsemani corresponding so precisely with Thomas Keating's death. But the surprising part is that I am neither Catholic nor Christian.

I am Jewish by birth, and spiritually inclusive by nature. Religious dogma packaged and sold by any of the world's faith traditions generally turns me off. And yet, I have spent much of my career as a translator, teacher, and author immersed in the teachings of the Christian mystics, a passion I shared with my friend Thomas Keating.

In fact, when I was writing my first book, a fresh translation of *Dark Night of the Soul* by John of the Cross, I drove ten hours from my home in Taos, New Mexico to Snowmass, Colorado to talk with Thomas about the text we both deeply loved, hoping to glean some insight I could convey to a conteporary spiritual audience, one that may or may not have been Christian. Thomas was the only other person I knew as who was obsessed with this text as I was. He had integrated these teachings into his bones.

"You can have one hour," his assistant informed me, accustomed to the many requests the aging priest received for private conversations, and determined to preserve his energy.

"Sold."

As it turned out, Thomas spent many hours with me that day, during which kindly friends slipped in and out with trays of tea and cookies to sustain us. As a result, the introduction to my translation of the *Dark Night* has Thomas's fingerprints all over it. He helped me to understand that when John spoke of "nada," he did not mean "nothing" in the conventional sense. He wasn't saying that we are unworthy or that our lives have no meaning compared to the greatness of God, but rather that when we allow our attachment to the "false self" to soften, when we wake up from the illusion of separation to the truth of our essential unity with God, we merge into that loving oneness. This is a mystical experience. And it belongs to everyone, Christian and non-Christian, believer and agnostic. It's a matter of "dying before you die," an aspirational value at the heart of most spiritual traditions, from the Eleusinian Mysteries to Sufism. This wisdom comes shining through this volume of Thomas Keating's teachings on death and dying, aptly titled *The Gift of Life*. The blessing of spiritual nothingness, as it turns out, is a state that can be touched by the disciplined practice of any contemplative method, such as Centering Prayer.

Contemplative practice teaches us to hold our preconceptions lightly and to willingly, even gratefully, die before we die.

Being with Thomas that day in Snowmass reminds me of a story about John of the Cross and Teresa of Avila. John would often visit Teresa in her community, and they would talk late into the night. Early one morning, when a young sister came into the convent kitchen to stir the ashes and get the fire going for breakfast, she found the two monastics where she had left them the night before, leaning close in ecstatic dialog. But now their chairs were a meter off the ground. I am not comparing myself to either saint in this scenario; I am affirming the power of any two souls who meet in loving exchange about spiritual things. The life-giving energy of soul friendship cannot be over-estimated. This is a blessing accessible to us all. We are called to cultivate beloved community, places that keep us accountable to ourselves and each other, and also celebrate the way the holy spirit pours into and through us whenever we gather to praise its presence.

I first met Thomas Keating at the Lama Foundation, the interspiritual community in the mountains of New Mexico where I lived as a young woman.

Later, I had the great fortune of gathering with Thomas and an intimate circle of younger contemplatives at the Snowmass Monastery Schoolhouse for a weekend dialog about the future of inter-mystical practice and its implications for a more awake and loving society. As my own vocation developed as a writer and speaker on the interconnections at the heart of the world's mystical traditions, Thomas cheered me on.

"As long as there is rigor!" he warned us about the interspiritual quest.

This admonition helped me stay strong and true, beyond the fluffy feel-good aspects of my explorations across traditions. I have had to keep letting go of my ideas of God to clear the way for a lived experience of God. To keep dying into a more direct and intimate communion with reality. I have Thomas Keating to thank for this impulse. And John of the Cross, too.

If you identify as "spiritual but not religious", or perhaps you're grounded in a faith other than Christianity, the pages of this little book may strike you as overly rooted in Christian language, as I admit it did me. I encourage us both to see beyond the religious idiom that was at the root of Thomas's faith to the vast and universal message he embraced and modeled. My personal friendship with Thomas is a testament to the power of his insights to resonate beyond religious boundaries—beyond interspirituality, even—and connect with the deepest hunger in our souls for union with the divine and peace among all beings. Pat Johnson, my lifelong friend and one of Thomas Keating's closest companions, said that Thomas always spoke openly about death, expressing that there was a big "cover-up" in contemporary American culture that tried to keep death at a distance. Embalming, funeral rituals, and other symptoms of "mythic membership" keep both the dying and those still living from having a sacred encounter with the mystery of death. Monks are laid in the chapel where they remain for three days after they die, "to give the soul time to catch up with the body," Pat explains, a custom Thomas Keating embraced.

May these pages help transform our fear of death and replace it with awe. I picture Thomas Keating crossing

the threshold into the next life with child-like won-
derment, arms outstretched, countenance radiant.
And I like to imagine that I, too, will enter like a child
into whatever is next.

INTRODUCTION

by Fr. Carl J. Arico

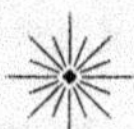

The original title of this nine-part series of interviews with Father Thomas Keating was *Death & Dying and the Unknowable God*. As we worked on the series, however, we began to realize that while the subject is death and dying, it is really about life. For that reason, we chose the title *The Gift of Life: Death & Dying, Life & Living*.

When people first heard we were planning a series on death with Father Thomas, many wondered what more could be said on this topic. What emerged from his wisdom was not simply reflections on death itself, but a call to change our attitude around both mind and heart about life as well as death. The series is a gift in helping us see death and dying within the larger reality of life and in light of the living presence of Christ.

As Father Thomas explains, when Centering Prayer reaches full consent to our nothingness—meaning the recognition that we are not the center of the world and that God is the source of our being—it becomes a profound preparation for dying. In this sense, it is already a kind of death: a death to the false self.

The false self is the way of seeing and living in which we experience ourselves as separate—separate from God, from others, and from our deepest truth. To consent to our nothingness does not mean self-negation; it means coming to realize that we are not in control, and that we are being held. This growing awareness is a preparation for death because it involves letting go of the false self.

At one point, Father Thomas asks a simple and penetrating question: What really dies? His answer is clear. What dies is the false self—the self we have constructed, often out of fear or misunderstanding, and which is out of harmony with the True Self, the person God created us to be.

Before reading further, take a moment to look carefully at the table of contents and consider the scope of what is explored here. I am often struck by how much time people spend planning for the future—meeting with financial planners, discussing security and possibility —while rarely preparing for the certainty of death. Why would we not prepare with the same care and attention?

As you read this book, I invite you to experience it as a process. Read slowly. Take time to reflect on what you have read, and allow space for prayer or quiet attention. Rest in the presence of God so that these insights may move from ideas into experience. Pay attention to what you feel as you read, especially what arises around death and dying and allow Christ's wisdom to meet you there.

When I speak at memorial gatherings, I often describe death as a second birth. Just as we once moved from the womb of our mother into a world we did not yet know, we will one day move from this life into another reality. Each transition is unchosen, and yet each is a continuation of life. Seen in this way, death is not an ending, but a passage.

Death and dying. Life and living. Death is only a moment in our lives. I invite you to enter fully into this book and its reflections. May it touch you deeply and support you in living and dying with greater trust, freedom, and peace.

PROLOGUE

Death is resurrection.
To accept death is to accept God.

I remember attending a funeral at the monastery in Snowmass of one of our elderly monks, Father Dan Kelleher. The bier on which he was laid stood between a very realistic cross on one side and the paschal candle on the other. These two objects are always present at a funeral that is held in a Catholic church. Maybe they are in front and behind or maybe at the two sides.

When I looked at the body from behind the altar as I was saying the Mass of the Resurrection, I was struck by the juxtaposition of the agonizing bronze body stretched on this very realistic cross, and on the other side, the paschal candle–tall because it was close to Easter. I could immediately intuit that death and resurrection, in the Christian perspective at least, can never be separated, and that in a very real sense, death is resurrection.

Death seems to be a process of transformation. The idea that something is dying needs to be investigated to see what it is. It is not we who are really dying but only the false self that is experiencing the end of its illusory view of life–our personal, homemade self, which has been the object of our efforts and is secretly present in virtually all our good deeds.

What's dying is not the deepest self, but our dependence and over-identification with the mental ego and its projects, and our cultural conditioning and over-identification with it, including our roles in life.

From this perspective, the dying process is the culmination or the peak of the whole development of the spiritual journey, in which total surrender to God involves the gift of life itself, as we know it. For that reason it's not really death, but life reaching out to a fullness that we can't imagine from this side of the dying process.

When Centering Prayer reaches the full consent to our nothingness, and when the closeness of God becomes a permanent experience, it is, of course, the perfect preparation for death, because it is death. One has already died to the false self in the Night of Sense, and in the Night of Spirit has died to the ego–and so, is there any self at all left? Nothing remains of the false self and the ego. And the True Self has been transcended.

So death is not the end of anything but the final completion of this process of becoming fully alive and manifesting the triumph of the grace of God in us.

STAGES OF DYING

*Dying is full integration
of body, soul, and spirit.*

Elisabeth Kübler-Ross serving in a Chicago hospital was the one who first investigated the process of dying with psychological acumen. She noticed several stages in the process, beginning with denial—an unwillingness to face the fact, even when the doctor says so, that one is in a dying condition. There's nothing by way of instruction, education, or life that prepares us for this eventuality.

Then there arise feelings of anger or rage, "How could this happen to me? Why? What do I do next? Will my friends still love me? Will they avoid me? Who is going to take care of me?" All of these may be acute and real concerns. Anger gradually subsides when we have to face death head-on.

Then comes the next stage, which is bargaining. Someone who has faith in the Ultimate Mystery might say, "Dear Lord, if you give me another few years to live, I'll become a Trappist" or "I'll give my estate to the poor." This is obviously not acceptance because there is still hope that God might somehow intervene and prolong life.

Bargaining is a struggle that involves trying to deal with God or to manage God in such a way as to get a reprieve of a few days, a few months, even a few years. The previous stages have brought the patient to a realization that death is actually happening and there is no way out of it, except bargaining.

When bargaining fails, depression may follow and be more or less deep. Some people may tend to withdraw, or sob, or feel abandoned. Of course, all of these dispositions are not a one-time event and can also interact with each other.

The final stage–acceptance–is not exactly a welcoming process. Acceptance can be a simple, "Oh God, I accept it!" One's emotional apparatus may not receive it graciously, depending on what the person's preparation for death, if any, has actually been. But what is happening is that divine love is so intense and so determined that it gradually leads the patient to an interior place where the devices for hiding from the certitude of death, or reacting, or bargaining are no longer possible.

This acceptance of the inevitable enables the transformation process to begin in real earnest and launches one towards the attitude of surrender, which is accepting the diminutions of self, as Teilhard de Chardin calls them.

In her book, *The Grace in Dying,* Kathleen Dowling Singh divides the dying process into three stages. The first stage she calls chaos, which covers the five stages identified by Kübler-Ross. "Chaos" could be any one of these stages or several put together, or it's the groaning and moaning of the separate self-sense and the mental-egoic consciousness that we have known from earliest childhood experiencing head-on the deprivation of what we relied upon, or hoped for, as the fulfillment of our human life.

Chaos corresponds pretty much to the variety of states that St. John of the Cross mentions in his book on the Dark Night of Sense and especially the Dark Night of Spirit in which even one's dependency on religious symbols and upon God is deeply challenged, and one may even have doubts about God's existence. The existential loneliness of death can be very hard but, for a lot of people, it seems to be the only way of shocking them at a deep enough level to allow the dynamic energies of the Divine Indwelling, the Holy Spirit, to start healing. Regeneration then begins to take place with the attitude of acceptance, however reluctant.

When acceptance has been well established, the stage of surrender occurs. The person and their psychic life are beginning to be renewed or revived, and the pain and psychological wounds of a lifetime are being healed as the patient not only accepts but really comes to terms with dying and begins to embrace the idea, maintaining peace and calm even in the midst of emotional ups and downs. These feelings are not stable qualities, but come and go at various levels, and keep moving toward to a sense of union and unity with God. Singh gives a number of examples that are very moving.

The final stage is unity consciousness or transcendence of the ego. This is not necessarily the ego's complete destruction, but its complete immobilizing–transcending might be the best word–of its idea of who we are and of the false self that we brought with us from early childhood and is the subject of purification.

Singh distinguishes near-death experience from near-ing-death experience. Nearing-death experience is a lengthy period that has these two characteristics of surrender and transcendence. (Chaos belongs to the earlier levels of adjustment to the process.) Surrender and transcendence are clear signs of the contemplative life.

Often dying patients show great interest in those that are with them, especially children and family, and are more concerned about them than about themselves. Often, too, in these final stages there is a sense of coming home, even of welcoming death and of experiencing the new life that is contained in death. In other words, these patients are experiencing, in the full sense of the term, inner resurrection. Sometimes care-takers can see that they are kind of glowing. According to Singh, if you have the interior eyes for this faith and love experience, you can see that something new has happened to them. A certain radiance in the body is sometimes evident, and they may speak of seeing beloved relatives who've preceded them in death and who have come to get them. There may even be some verbal exchange, and the patients smile in recognition. The closer they get to death, the happier they seem to become. At the end they sometimes reach out a welcoming hand toward whoever has come.

About a day or two before dying, one patient said, "I never knew that dying was so wonderful!" That story reminded me of one of the early members of Contemplative Outreach who had run a retreat house in a local parish in New Hampshire, Sister Mary Anne Laughlin. When she was dying, she was surrounded by many friends to whom she kept saying, "I never knew death could be so much fun!"

One of the leaders of Contemplative Outreach at the time of these lectures is dying with terminal cancer. He is using his remaining time to travel with his wife and enjoy their long and special relationship. He wrote us saying, "Whether it's here or there, it is all the same!" By "here or there," he means that God has become a transcending presence for him whether he dies or lives. This is the kind of integral freedom that characterizes the final stage of transformation in Christ. It's the stage that St. John of the Cross would call not only spiritual marriage, but the furthest development and maturation of it.

All this can take place in a short time–a year, six months, or maybe a month or two. Singh says that she sees it happening even in people who only have a week or a few days–even hours! –though in this short time the process is not as clear as it is in a more extended experience.

The highest quality in the transformative process of our dying is to experience inner resurrection, which is the Trinity within us. Thus, in our sufferings there is a hidden inner and divine work going on that is relentless and challenging. Its purpose is to heal all the wounds of the soul so that we can open completely to God and feel the regenerating, powerful forces that we may have been separated from for all or most of our earthly life concerns. Anger gradually subsides when we have to face death head-on.

SUFFERING

Suffering leads to wisdom,
when it is accepted.

At certain parts of the dying process, the physical suffering, no matter how great it may be, may not be commensurate with the spiritual suffering that is going on as the ego is asked to let go of its memories, attachments, and concerns for the future of its loved ones whom it can no longer take care of or protect. This suffering is especially deep in the case of parents with young children they have to leave behind. As the person nears death, it looks as though they're having a terrible struggle consenting, or letting go of life; or they fear what is to follow, or they may even fear God, or punishment, depending on the nature of their religious and cultural background.

The same sort of state occurs in extended periods of the Dark Night of the Spirit in St. John of the Cross. In these writings you find a classical description of what to ordinary folks would seem like impossible states of consciousness for devout persons who wonder whether they can be saved, and at times feel rejected by God.

You can't very well tell them they're in the Dark Night unless they would find some consolation in that. In any case, they don't have to be told…they're in it! They *are* it, and so their sufferings can be almost unbearable. In Kübler-Ross' stages of dying, depression that is close to despair can occur when the dying process is quite far advanced, just before the emergence of acceptance. Acceptance doesn't take away the suffering, but changes the attitude towards it.

In regard to suffering, everything depends on the attitude of the patient to what seems to be unbearable, unreasonable, irrational, and all the ways we complain about God not answering our prayers, or not taking care of us, or not providing us with a peaceful and happy death. We may get angry at God, and some people may even reject God at that point. Job came close to that disposition in his mounting difficulties. There may be extreme pain when the patient feels they are not getting a fair deal from God. "Why me?" But, the "Why me?" is the basic question that suffering and God's permission of it has in mind: "Who are you actually?" The answer is that the human condition involves pain by the very nature of this creation and of earthly living, which is somewhat precarious–to put it mildly. Pain can be modified by modern medicine to acceptable degrees, if one has access to good medical care including appropriate medication.

Suffering arises when we resist the pain or circumstances of life. These challenge our idea of ourselves and undermine the way that we understood our life and its meaning for us, which is now empty of the promises it may have held out for us in childhood and early adult life.

Suffering in the dying process is the psychological consequence of pain and the inevitability of death, which is now close and impossible to avoid. There may be issues in the history of the patient that are very painful–people that they have ceased to speak to, parents that they have forgotten about, friends who have betrayed them, or children who are too busy about their own affairs to be concerned. Then there are the beloved ones who *are* concerned but who can do nothing and for whom the patient can't do anything either because they are barely able to handle their own suffering.

And yet, as sometimes happens in deep prayer, especially in the context of the Dark Night of the Spirit, when one has reached the full extent of one's endurance and nothing is working–out of nowhere comes the consoling presence of God, which can put the person into a sense of great peace or lead them into a transcendence of their present stage of consciousness into one of total acceptance and surrender. When there is complete surrender, one's personal suffering is not really suffering anymore.

When accepted, suffering leads to wisdom, which is the perception of the divine goodness and purpose in everything that happens. Wisdom, peace, and faith–that is to say, perfect trust in God–transform suffering into–I won't quite say 'joy'–but give it a meaning that takes away resistance and one can then see a value in one's suffering that is...well, God-like.

When my mother was dying, she reached a state where she couldn't keep her dentures in her mouth. She was praying that she might die, and she kept complaining, "Why can't I die?" She felt that she wasn't doing anybody any good. How she looked was important to her, and she didn't want to be a burden to anyone. These human considerations are very poignant. I remember a Mass I was saying in her bedroom. After the *Agnes Dei,* the prayer just before the priest receives Communion, she prayed in a loud voice that expressed a great deal of frustration, "Please, Lord, let me die! Please let me die!" It was sad to see her in such a state. Thus, instead of wanting to live, those who are suffering may experience a great desire to end it. They can't stand the diminishments of self anymore and feel there is no reason for living; they are just alone with their pain. Most relatives feel more or less helpless and do not know how to help.

Maybe the most they can do is hold the hand of the loved one or embrace her, provided, of course, they can get through all the tubes that may be prolonging life. At some point, there is a shift into a new state of consciousness in which there is an increased awareness of the Holy Spirit, or of Christ. The form of this awareness reflects one's religious convictions and is congenial to the particular psychology of each person.

Death is really not death, but an introduction into a life of union with God that is beyond anything we can imagine. We can't describe this in ordinary language, but only in symbolic language that points to an experience. It's a way of expressing the inexpressible–the inexpressible being the actual feeling of being embraced by God or of being in the divine milieu, so to speak, where there are many mansions. The negativities of the dying process are balanced by the beginning of a power to enjoy the eternal life that is dawning.

Thus, interior and external suffering are not incompatible with peace and joy. On one level it may be something we don't want; but on another, we see a benefit that we do want, and these differing emotions are going on at once. A resolution of opposites is taking place.

In all this suffering there is a dimension that doesn't appear in the sense order, at least not at once. The patient experiences a shift. Those who are working closely with the dying person can see that something has definitely changed, and they may report that the person is in great peace. They have passed through the major stages in the dying process and are coming out the other side.

There may still be suffering and sometimes more than the patient can articulate. But at the deepest level, it's not blowing them away because they have the further intuition that their suffering is meaningful, that it is providing the energy of love that is transforming the whole body in varying degrees, depending on the intensity and purity of the love that is there. Christ's example is the major example. There's no self-centeredness in transcendence or in the transformative process, as there was no concern for self in Christ, but a compassion that is willing to take on the sufferings of others, without regard for oneself.

Death really is resurrection. Rising from the dead, as Christ did, is inherent in the very process of suffering.

JUDGMENT & MERCY

*Death is the last judgment
for each of us.*

For all practical purposes, death is the last judgment for each of us, as far as we're concerned in our personal life. Scripture indeed, says in one place, that after death comes the judgment. It seems, therefore, that there are two judgments: the personal one and later the final one in which Christians believe that the resurrection of the dead will take place.

But what sort of bodies will people have before that time? Because that may be a long time away, we may be only at the very beginning of the human potential. It may take millennia to complete the transformation of humanity into the gloried Body of Christ in which the divine presence is operative fully in every part.

One of the things that disturbs a lot of people as they approach death is whether they could have done better with their lives, or whether, if they had another chance, they would do things differently. Sometimes they have been through experiences where they felt they did something that weighs heavily on their conscience and for which they really haven't forgiven themselves.

A part of the process of letting go is to forgive ourselves and to trust God enough that if we are sorry for our misbehaviors, God has completely forgotten about them and would prefer that we would too. To live in the present moment means that the past has been integrated into who we are now. To think back would be a foolish thing to do because we can never judge the dispositions that we had then with how we now would judge certain behaviors. It's an injustice to ourselves to indulge guilt feelings that are the result of seeing in the present the serious harm that we did in the past, but which we didn't perceive at all, or at least very little, at the time.

To love oneself is to be as merciful and compassionate to ourselves as we try to be towards others. Can we really forgive others until we have learned to forgive ourselves? A lot of the things that hurt us profoundly we project upon others. Hence, if we haven't fully forgiven ourselves for our failings and sins, we are not likely to be fully forgiving of others.

Part of acceptance is just to be still and surrender to God knowing that all God wants is our love. For Christians, God's attitude toward sinners is there staring us in the face in the Parable of the Prodigal Son. If you have problems with the past, read that parable over again because what it reveals is God's attitude towards our misconduct and perhaps even our resentment toward God because of it. The Prodigal Son in the parable used up all the money for his father's old age in his profligate life. The father is represented as waiting for him to appear–and scanning the horizon to see if he is on his way back. The Prodigal Son came home for selfish reasons. He was chiefly interested in getting enough to eat. The father rushes out to meet him and gives him everything he had before, and calls on the household to celebrate his return.

This is the Christian understanding of God's attitude towards the sinner. There are consequences to misbehavior that may linger, but these become means of integrating motives for humility into our relationship with God, and can actually bring us to a stage of greater holiness than if we had never sinned.

If a dying person is afraid of judgment for past misdeeds, tell the patient to forget it! Your company in this lonely journey may help the person to get beyond self-centered concerns and to accept the gift of total forgiveness that God is offering.

It doesn't take much to let go. It doesn't take much time. What takes time is trying to decide whether to let go or not! Letting go is not difficult. It's painful, but the pain is coming from the illness that is being healed. You find this symbolized in the description of Lazarus in St. John's Gospel, who suffers from a serious sickness that Jesus at first doesn't seem interested in healing. The sisters of Lazarus sent word to him, saying, very respectfully, "If you had been here, our brother would not have died." But that implies, "*Why weren't you here,* when you were present with all those other people you rescued from illness that you didn't even know?" But their love was at such a point that they knew that there was something important going on here.

Jesus couldn't heal Lazarus from his illness since it represented the false self, the only cure for which is death. But once that had taken place, the real Lazarus with his True Self was called forth from the tomb–that is, from the corruption of his false self system–into the new life and into the new creation. The dying process is a process created by God to release the divine energies within the soul that have always been there. It is better called an "awakening" rather than a discovery because it isn't something that you can go and look for. It is within you. We are not able to perceive it as long as the mental ego is dominating our consciousness with its limited perspectives.

The stages of dying are also stages that can occur in the unfolding of the Christian mystical journey and, doubtless, in other transformative processes. When they reach the point of integration, the patient has finally become aware of who he or she really is and can say with the writer of the Psalms: "I will dwell in the house of the Lord all the days of my life." As Jesus said, "in my house there are many mansions"–that is to say, many levels of divine union appropriate to the various inhabitants. The beauty of the divine house is not in the details but in the presence of the Great Awareness and its spaciousness, which has no end and no boundaries. This spaciousness is our participation in the divine life. It doesn't obliterate the details of our uniqueness or basic human identity, but all possessive attitudes are purged away and put to rest. The True Self, or "new creation," as Saint Paul calls it, has replaced the life of mental egoistic activities no matter how much they may have dominated throughout one's life.

AFTER DEATH

What is left? The True Self,
the image of God in us.

As we are dying, it becomes clear that a number of influences on our free will and judgment that we make about ourselves and our decisions in light of them are no longer functioning. What is left is the awareness of the True Self, that is, the image of God in us, which we may have become acquainted with through the practice of contemplation—or may not have discovered until this moment. But now that it is free of all those influences, our spirit is able to make a decision to accept God. It's more free of obstacles to doing this than it has ever been, because those obstacles have been dissolved in the dissolution of the organs that provided that information.

At this time, one sees exactly what one's state is: whether one is ready for perfect love and to join the Communion of Saints, or whether one needs to be enlightened as to those things in oneself that are still self-centered and opposed to the agapic love that is characteristic of divine life. To enter heaven without that love might be to feel out of place–like coming late to a dinner party or to which you weren't really invited! We may be able to crash a party in this world, but the heavenly dinner party is not crashable. What that means is that our spirit will embrace whatever its proper state requires, given its spiritual development and integration at the moment of death.

This is why it is a good idea to accept the purification process, which is also the healing process, while still in this world, and why such commitment to the spiritual journey has accrued over the centuries as preparation for eternal life.

PURGATORY

The same process of healing and liberation takes place in the Night of Spirit, which is the equivalent of purgatory according to John of the Cross. Someone who has been through that night, he writes, can enter directly into heaven.

In the purification process, one keeps seeing aspects of ourselves that are self-centered or overly dependent on external circumstances, groups, or expectations. As a result, one is constantly taking more and more responsibility for one's behavior. Facing the dark side of our personality, or the "shadow," as Jung calls it, is regarded in transpersonal circles and in all the religious spiritual traditions as an essential part of the journey. The purification of selfishness and opening to compassion and pure love initially cause us pain because we are programmed to do it our own way. Purification involves a "letting go" that takes time to fully establish. The process of letting go is obviously central in the dying process too–only there, you don't have to create it yourself because it is provided by circumstances.

Purgatory is the process of getting into these dispositions so that you can surrender. That's all it is. It is not a punishment. It is not a course in revenge, or of justice, or of canon law. These are all static concepts that come from the rational view of God.

Sometimes people have various levels of guilt feelings and feel a need to make reparation in the sense of payment, analogous to going to prison to pay a debt to society. But this is not the divine attitude at all. God has forgiven sins–"taken away"–the sins of the world. To ask for forgiveness is the movement of love, not a bargaining process.

HELL

The concept of hell has disturbed people for centuries and in some Christian traditions has even terrified people, especially as they approach the ultimate hour of confrontation with the reality of death. This is the most horrendous sanction that has ever been thought of for misdeeds.

The mystery of hell is presented in Jesus's teaching and needs to be researched prayerfully and deeply to try to grasp what it means in an era, such as we are beginning to live in, of profound psychological insight about how the human psyche works in particular circumstances and in relation to the context of one's whole life and the influences that have formed our concept of self or ego.

Father Karl Rahner, one of the great theologians at the time of the Second Vatican Council, taught that Christians must believe in hell, but he adds that this doesn't necessarily mean that anyone is *there!* The concept of hell as fire and brimstone, the eternal loss of God, and the constant torment of memories comes across as unrealistic today. Pope Benedict XVI suggested that we might perceive hell as primarily a state of consciousness, rather than a place.

There seems to be a contradiction in the traditional concept of hell: How, if God wills all to be saved, is it possible for some not to be saved? Theology and its reflections are at pains to make sure that God's freedom is always maintained. But how to explain this freedom when humans have freedom? The real answer is that reason can't understand this.

We make our own hell through our emotional programs for happiness that can't possibly work, and which create intense depression when they are frustrated over a long period of time. When we get what we want, the project doesn't deliver. It's essentially impermanent. It's not what we thought.

So is hell eternal *actually*? Or is hell eternal *psychologically*–that is to say, a psychological state that feels as if it will never end?

Descriptions of the eternity of hell are similar to expressions of the experience that occurs during the Dark Nights, when the sense of time is overwhelmed by the experience of the moment, whether of consolation or of desolation, which doesn't leave room for succession or chronology. If there is time in eternity, it's certainly different from what we understand as time in this world.

HEAVEN

A few words about how we conceive of heaven or what is revealed about it–which seems to be "not much!" The higher stages of contemplative prayer in the spiritual journey are often described as an anticipation of heaven. It's not about thinking, that's for sure, because the brain is dead. It's about the joy of participating in the attributes of God, namely compassion, forgiveness, reconciliation, freedom, joy. The beatitude consists in being completely free to love God without the limitations of self-reflection or the commentaries that we have had to put up with in this life. The false self and ego are dead, so we see life and other people only through the eyes of God, which is to see them truly and much more beautifully than we have been able to see them before. Everything is what it is–God manifesting God's self. It's the celebration of being.

Heaven can be described as a place where we get accustomed to the divine energies and learn how to surf them, so to speak. We allow God to happen within us and to fulfill whatever further vocation given to us as servants of God, such as messengers of God's good-will to people still in this life on earth.

The nature of being is to grow, so heaven is not the end of the spiritual journey, but the beginning of a new life. Whatever choices there are, heaven is primarily the home of total self-surrender.

As Catherine of Genoa said, "There is no me but God." But that doesn't take away the fact that from a rational point of view, we can't resolve the opposites—that God is all, and yet there is still us; there is unity and diversity. The reality of God into which we are invited is the world where the opposites are resolved in the higher consciousness that is both at once. The uncreated experience of God is the essence of heaven, and this is a state of consciousness more than a place.

THE COMMUNION OF SAINTS

The cells in a human body are a magnificent image of each of the individual persons in the Mystical Body of Christ. To be a healthy cell contributes to the growth and development of this body, which Paul calls the "full age of Christ." This is what we are waiting for–the development of this corporate body, which is all humanity, but especially those who are incorporated in the transformative process and who have answered the invitation in their respective religions to be transformed.

The Communion of Saints is not just a nice association like a club. It's the whole inter-relatedness and the common sharing of human life and the common contribution of each generation to try to further the project of the divine life–not only to pass it on, at least to the next generation, but also to fulfill the particular role to which the Spirit calls us and works through us. In philosophical psychology, the soul fills every part of the body–every cell, we would now say. The Holy Spirit is also present in every cell of the body, including the diseased members, which need the healing of the members who are in better health. Everybody is collaborating, or should be collaborating.

This union and unity are so complete that the full meaning–the potential–of the doctrine of the Communion of Saints points to such dispositions as universal compassion and a willingness to prefer the good of others to our own–which is to go beyond the commandment to love our neighbor as ourselves.

So the human or rational considerations of competi-
tion, all of which come from the false self and the ego,
are for the birds! Those dispositions have no future in
the Communion of Saints. When the brain, with its
habits of thought, disintegrates, our spirit has for the
first time complete freedom to choose God without
interference and to surrender to God. Surrender is
the dispossession of everything for the love of God.

WHAT HAPPENS AFTER DEATH?

Questions about what happens in the next life ought
to take account of what Paul says–that "we are now the
children of God, but no one can imagine what God has
prepared for those who love him." It might be good to
take those words seriously and make time in daily life
just to be quiet and still.

THE CROSS

Total self-surrender enables Christ
to renew all the mysteries
of his life in each of us.

When we look at the cross, what we are looking at is infinite love–God's great love. The cross is an invitation to join in God's project of bringing the whole human family into the totally gratuitous love, joy, and bliss of sharing the life of the Trinity. The cross gives a hint of what the degree of love and what the level of surrender might be.

The ultimate meaning of the cross is not just to redeem humanity from sin or to manifest God's great love for us, but to invite us in the most powerful way possible by showing God's willingness to do anything to bring us into the life of the Trinity, to fill us with its joy, and to invite us into the home of all that exists. From the perspective of self-surrender, pain is joy and joy is pain.

Perhaps it might be helpful just to list briefly the symbols of the ascending spiritual meanings of the cross. These symbols become more evident as we pass from stage to stage in the transforming process.

SYMBOLS AND MEANINGS OF THE CROSS

NAKED CROSS

The naked cross is a symbol of the human condition. We are unable to regress to the irresponsibility of beasts and unable to go forward into the perfect freedom of divine union and unity. We find ourselves literally crucified between heaven and earth in a place of great pain, confusion, anxiety, and helplessness that might be called our participation in the human condition.

BODY ON THE CROSS

When we put the body of the divine human being, Jesus Christ, on the cross, this is the symbol that God identifies completely with the human condition, even to the point of experiencing it fully himself. In the process of doing so, Christ manifests the immense love of God, which could have redeemed us from our guilt feelings and deliberate faults, without having to put God's Son through the extreme sacrifice of the cross. Many theologians–St. Bonaventure and Duns Scotus, for example–regarded the redemption of human beings as not a sufficient motive to bring about the redemptive sacrifice of Christ, the divine-human being. This becoming human is not required by the sins of humanity because God could have forgiven all sin without requiring that sacrifice.

SACRIFICE

The sacrifice itself is the annihilation of sin from the perspective of guilt and shame.

TAKING AWAY OF ALL SIN

The fourth is the taking away and the healing of the radical wounds of the un-evolved state.

DIVINE LOVE / DIVINE INVITATION

The fifth is the ultimate expression of God's invitation to humanity to divine union. In St. Bonaventure's scheme of things, the cross represents an expression of divine love and a revelation of the Father, which takes that love to its most extreme or comprehensive level. We are invited to participate in the redemption of the world, not just to look at the cross, but to become one with the suffering Christ–in other words, to take part in this infinite agapic love that is beyond love, beyond human consolation, beyond the state of spiritual marriage. This is the level of unity consciousness in which the divine capacities for love are offered to us to whatever degree we are capable of and willing to receiving them.

If we accept this invitation, we are accepting not so much physical suffering or the sufferings of the dark nights but accepting God just as God is. This is to accept the fact that the greatest experience of God is no experience. But that experience is the greatest one there is!

Our total self-surrender enables Christ to renew the mysteries of his life on earth in each of us and in our particular form of life. It's not so much the magnitude of our service or the amount of suffering we endure, but the amount of divine love that we bring to the details of everyday life.

CHRIST AS SIN

The sixth symbol is a further divine invitation as you look upon the cross. I would think one isn't able to perceive it, at least in a way that would motivate us, unless one has made a certain progress in the stages of consciousness beyond the rational level. We see ourselves invited to identify with Christ as sin. There is a double identification here. We are not just identifying with Christ's suffering; we are identifying with Christ who is suffering because he has taken upon himself the sin of the whole human race from the beginning of time to the end. Now that we have perceived these symbols and are moved by the extent of God's love, we are invited to participate with Christ in the healing of the human race itself.

DESCENT INTO HELL

The descent into hell might be considered the seventh symbol and revelation of the cross. This means hitting bottom, going to the absolute limit of humility and the dispossession of self.

Only in this case, it's the divine disposition in so far as it can divest itself of its infinite goodness and plunge into the absolute abyss of possibility in human freedom, which is the rejection of God's goodness and love. So this is the moment of redemption, as Hans Urs von Balthasar sees it, in his marvelous description of the psychological or spiritual dispossession of Christ, of every shred of visible divinity. It is so deep that it expresses moments when, from our side of the identification, we experience ourselves as capable of any evil and of total powerlessness to respond to God's love. We wish to be annihilated so as not to contribute any more to Christ's sufferings.

To do everything for love, to be one with Christ's love, to allow the love of God to inspire us in every detail of life without thinking about it, but simply renewing our will to accept the present moment, dying into the present moment and its content by letting go of our own will–these are all implied in this symbol of joining Christ at the moment, not of his glory, but of his identification with sin and the consequences of sin. It is the willingness to be nothing, the willingness to be the opposite of God, the willingness to be whatever our share of the human condition is and to be completely transformed into Christ. It's a letting go of self in the most radical way and the death of the ego.

RESURRECTION

This is a moment of interior resurrection, which Christ celebrated in a special way on the day of his Resurrection, when he visited the room where the apostles had gathered together out of fear of the authorities. He entered through locked doors and said to them, "Peace be with you." He established them in peace and then communicated to them the Holy Spirit, the supreme gift of the Father and the Son and the decisive triumph of love over sin. After breathing on the apostles–breath being the symbol of the Spirit–he said, "Receive the Holy Spirit."

To be totally open and willing to receive the fullness of the Spirit is the proper disposition for transformation. What is important at this point is not our self-initiated activity, but our humility based on our having tasted to the depths the lack of integrity and the possibility of all evil that is inherent in the freedom of choice of our human nature as well as its capacity to receive God. We receive the Spirit in the degree that we have been divested of the false self and have allowed it to die with Christ. Now we are ready to rise with Christ with all the attributes that are present in the divine human being, and through the Holy Spirit, to live ordinary human life in a divine way, thus manifesting the Father in all our actions and relationships.

ASCENSION

The final development or symbol of the cross is, of course, the Ascension, which is our return to the Source and our entrance into the bosom of the Father. We enter into the house of God as a permanent state of consciousness, even in this life, by being always aware of the divine ground within us and of the spaciousness that has no end.

I suppose you could certainly see other symbols of the cross. We can never come to the bottom of the abyss of meaning, of inspiration, or of experience that is contained not just in thinking about the cross or meditating on it, but in going through the crucifixion oneself and coming out the other side through the experience of inner resurrection and union with Christ. That is the basic principle of apostolic love, which is the love that the apostles received at Pentecost, and which is the true and fullest source of evangelization.

This love is both visibly and invisibly expressed, and brings about the transformation of society and any number of important developments for the human species that are hidden from the usual sources of knowledge and discussion.

We might see the process of near-death and dying in terms of these symbols. That is, a person is moving—maybe not in this order, exactly–through participating in suffering and in death in a way that enables them to perceive the meaning of the cross with new eyes. Death is resurrection and resurrection is death. It's our limitations from a rational point of view that seem to see contradiction there.

THE MYSTERY OF GOD

We have the capacity to know
God by relationship.

Who am I? What is the meaning of life? Is there a God? If so, what's he–or she–like? Is God personal or impersonal? All humanity shares these questions even if through different cultural expressions.

The questions that appear even in the Book of Genesis suggest that these great questions of life are a mystery to us. The consciousness of humans and its physiological basis in the brain enable the possessor to have the capacity to know God by way of relationship, if not by way of rational definition. To know God through the experience of relationship leads to a sense of belonging to the universe and inspires a reverence for the Creator.

One's starting point for seeking the Unknown and Unknowable God makes a big diference. In the spiritual journey, time is designed to provide the space for different spiritual experiences. The journey follows a certain order. It is not entirely chaotic, although we may experience certain parts of it that way. As the spiritual life evolves, there is a time for ritual, for vocal prayer, and for relating to God more or less as another human being–or at least as a God who is sympathetic to the human condition. There's a time, in other words, for a fairly exoteric, that is, a fairly external observance, and this seems to involve most of the people who identify with a particular religion. They fulfill certain external demands without understanding what is involved or what their purpse might be.

It's only when the externals of the journey begin to be interiorized by whatever means–and there are many–that they may then experience a great devotion to the saints. They look for help from departed beloveds, or from saints or sages–and later they may get more attracted to the angels.

In the spiritual journey, there seems to be a time for saints, a time for angels, and then a time for a deepening relationship with Christ. There is the possibility of spiritual friendship as Christ becomes the center of our lives and we try to imitate and to become Christ. This development is moving towards spiritual marriage. Christ as bridegroom, lover, or beloved begins to preoccupy our devotional life. He leads us to the Trinity, and then to each member of the Trinity, and finally to unity with the Trinity.

There is no possessive attitude in Divine Love; it gives itself completely. In the Trinity, this is delightful. This is what beatitude is. It is a love beyond any love that we can imagine. It is a love that is actually and really being given all the time, so that it is like an enormous river of Divine Love flowing among the relationships in the Trinity and throughout creation forever.

Nothing is more delightful than to receive and to give back this infinite agape, the pure love of God, which is totally non-possessive. It is into this non-possessive attitude that the dying process is designed to draw us because one gives up all one's possessions, including eventually the body and one's loved ones, and one is reduced to no particular thing, that is, to nothingness. When one not only accepts this, but surrenders to it, one enters into the eternal flow of Divine life.

One's relationship with God needs to be flexible enough to be open to breakthroughs and to change. All relationships with God are gradually absorbed into ever higher and deeper penetrations into the mystery and unity with the Ultimate Reality.

God presents in two ways or, more exactly, in one way–and is simply present in the other. This distinction is called created grace and uncreated grace in Christian theology. Created grace involves all means of transformation, including our personal experience of God. Uncreated grace is unity with the Unknowable God. This is the God who actually is, who was, and always will be.

The Ground of Being is an adequate term as a pointer to it. Certainly Meister Eckhart thinks so. That-Which-Is cannot be experienced. So the greatest experience of God is no experience–not because it isn't an experience, but because there are no faculties in us that are commensurate to experiencing it. Still, the Ultimate Reality is known in a certain way through faith, which knows that it is unknowable, a knowledge that requires our consent to the diminishment of all our other relationships with God. It sees God in everything and that ultimately everything is God, and there is no other.

Rudolph Otto's words *mysterium tremendum et fascinans* express it well. This Latin phrase acknowledges the tremendous mystery, or the overwhelming mystery, or the mystery that can't be penetrated, or the unknowable mystery. At the same time, the Ultimate Mystery is utterly fascinating and desirable, and the longing to experience and possess it is deeply implanted in human nature. Despite the clutter of other purposes in life, we are never quite at peace without developing this ultimate relationship. Thus, the *mysterium tremendum et fascinans* is a necessary factor in the process of surrendering to the mystery that is not understandable to us, but is *determined* to share with us the beauty, goodness, freedom, compassion, and forgiveness of God as gratuitous gifts.

The whole approach to God that one has used up to that point has to go through a 180-degree shift. We thought of ourselves as seeking God–and we needed to open to this deeper dimension of our being that is beyond reason. We had to exhaust the possibilities of knowing God that reason can provide with the help of religion and the religious symbols that enable God to peep, you might say, or to slip through the cracks in sacred words, symbols, and gestures, and to give us the sense that there is more to this life than meets the eye. The eye of faith penetrates the external senses and ordinary events and sees God in everything. It sees not just the particular particle, so to speak, but also the source of the particle, which resides with it together at the same time. Similarly, God is both distinct and indistinct from everything at the same time, including ourselves.

Belief systems refer to the way that faith is explained in a rational way so that God can be grasped by people who don't have an actual relationship with God as yet, but who are open to it and who are developing through various disciplines or practices this dimension of their deeper selves.

Traditionally, meditation in its conceptual form, which we call contemplation in the Christian tradition, is perhaps the easiest way to access the spiritual level of our being. This is the divine presence with its creative energy and its continuing accompaniment as our human development advances. Cultivating this relationship with God moves from acquaintanceship to friendship to union, as in a human relationship of growing friendship.

When in Centering Prayer, we present our limited being just as it is, with all our faults, confusion, uncertainties, guilt feelings, shame, and the emotional wounds that we bring with us from early childhood (some of which have been repressed into the unconscious because they were too painful to face at the time), the Divine Presence begins to emerge from time to time in ways that are proportionate to a person's capacity to handle such relationships.

The *mysterium tremendum* is not easily experienced in its fullness without a physical as well as mental preparation because if the nervous system is not accustomed to a certain level of this energy and suddenly moves to some kind of theophany of God, it could be blown away. (If you got the full blast, you might be reduced to a grease spot!)

With great care and love, God makes sure to hide the intensity of the Divine Presence behind the external senses and behind our faults, which enable us to keep a certain distance from God out of sheer respect. We hesitate to appear before God with all the things in us that we feel are opposite or inappropriate to God. Everything is carefully balanced as our spiritual life advances so that we can experience more and more levels of relationship with God both in prayer and in action.

The spiritual journey is a process that happens to us. We don't do it. The Mystery unfolds of itself. The Christian mystical tradition is a process that is appropriate for those devoting themselves to seeking the Mystery that is at once awesome and irresistible. These seekers are motivated by the desire to know, to serve, and to do the will of this immense goodness–a presence that becomes more and more intimate and tender.

THEOLOGICAL FOUNDATION

What is your starting point for theology?

In most of the Christian traditions there is a reliance upon reason to try to explain the existence of God—and when that is not possible, at least to study the mystery of God from the perspective of metaphysics, which actually comes from Aristotle rather than from Scripture. Maybe they relied upon Aristotle because they didn't have the resources in the Middle Ages that we have today. There weren't many books, although they did a terrific job copying the books they had, including Aristotle. So, one may wonder what sources ordinary priests and bishops had to rely on in their understanding of the Christian mystery.

When it came to explaining the Trinity and the Incarnation–the #1 and #2 of the Christian mysteries –these early Christian thinkers used language that tended not do justice to the whole mystery. This mystery has both a metaphysical aspect and, to judge by Scripture, a relational one. This is God's invitation to every individual, especially through the events beginning with the Incarnation–an extraordinary invitation to the human species all together and one by one to consent to God's invitation to share the divine life and, as Paul says, to become God's children and heirs to the Kingdom.

What is the Christian starting point for theological reflection on these mysteries? According to Father Christos Yannaras, a distinguished Greek Orthodox theologian of our time, the primary division between Eastern and Western Christianity is the profoundly distinct starting point for theological reflection. In *Person and Eros*, he writes that the West chose the metaphysics of Aristotle and the Greek philosophers as the starting point for understanding human anthropology and the transmission of the faith of the apostles.

In contrast, the Greek Fathers of the Church–Gregory of Nyssa, Gregory Nazianzen, Basil, and especially

Maximus the Confessor–emphasized the Scriptural basis for theology where the Trinity is revealed, not through philosophy, however valuable that may be as a way of looking at reality, but through revelation. Father Yannaras emphasizes the fact that the Greek Fathers deliberately rejected the approach of the West, and concludes that Eastern and Western Christianity can never be brought together in unity while the West maintains its starting point for theology in the metaphysics and anthropology of the great Greek philosophers.

In Western Christianity the attempt to *explain* the Trinity tends to dominate. Human reason, by its very nature, attempts to dominate what it thinks about–to take it in, and to make it understandable–whereas the Eastern approach has maintained the mystery of God that can only be revealed through revelation. This is the meaning of the icon in Orthodox spirituality that somehow transmits the experience of God rather than the thought of God.

Thinking tries to dominate God and bring the divine mysteries into our capacity to understand and comprehend them. The Eastern Fathers of the Church, on the other hand, insisted on experience itself as the communication of God, based on the fact that the Trinity is not revealed in philosophy but in the scriptures. This is an extremely important point in ecumenical dialogue between Eastern and Western theologians.

The basic question for that dialogue is: what is the starting point for theology in the first place? If it's about dominating the truths of faith by forcing them into a set of philosophical principles, God is looked upon in that frame of reference, as in the religions that are monotheistic. But as Raimon Panikkar, a great theologian of our time, has pointed out, this perspective doesn't do sufficient justice to the presence of the mystery in the Christian religion. The development of the rational faculties seems to have been a process that has led step-by-step to the exaltation of reason and of rationalizing about the mysteries of faith, to the point that the Enlightenment and then the technological culture that has emerged from it, is really based on the frame of mind that sees reality as something that the human mind can comprehend and dominate.

Without giving enough emphasis to transformation as the starting point for the discussion, can we possibly solve the questions of our time, which are the result of an over-identification with the philosophical approach and reliance on the capacity of reason to explain and convince people of the integrity of faith?

Monotheism is not about relationship. It tends to emphasize the transcendence of God, so that to operate out of that starting point and build theology on it leads you, as Panikkar points out, into several contradictions. One is that you have to avoid pantheism, and the other is that you have to uphold the freedom of God and the gratuity of grace. Neither of these can be thoroughly purged with a monotheistic view. The Jewish religion, of course, triumphed in its time in overcoming the pluralism of gods, but in doing so, became a monotheistic religion with these inherent contradictions.

Without the Trinitarian revelation of Scripture, it is virtually impossible to understand the cross as the greatest revelation of God and to trust God's invitation to divine union.

The Eastern Orthodox approach needs greater study and research by Western theologians and authorities, which is beginning to happen with the introduction of inter-religious dialogue. But at some point, because this approach is so deep, the dialogue will involve a huge challenge. As Father Yannaras points out, the whole development of the culture of Europe and the western world is rooted in the principle of the domination of nature rather than service and relationship. This is an extremely important issue. As we study the differences between these two alternatives, it may dawn on us that we have yet to recognize the real problem, which is not about this or that doctrine, but about the choice of rooting the whole theological program in the metaphysics of Aristotle or in the revelation of Scripture.

To sum up this great issue: Are we going to start our reflections with a philosophical model that leads to abstract attributes about God? Scholastic philosophy has brought us insights into the Divine as omniscient, all powerful, and utterly transcendent. This is true up to a point, and of great value, but is it the way Scripture presents God? In Scripture, God is represented primarily as relationship, as seeking us and opening to us every possible relationship including sharing and becoming one with the One God.

COMING HOME

If we really trust God,
we don't have a care in the world.

The dying process is the culmination, or the peak, of the whole development of the spiritual journey, in which the total surrender to God involves the gift of life itself as we know it. But the actual manifestation of the process is going to be according to God's will, and in different people will differ according to their vocation. The fullness of redemption is the capacity to be completely transformed in order to consent to the taking over of our entire being by the Divine Goodness. This is why it is necessary to get people into a practice that can move them beyond the limitations of their reason and their inclination to comment from this level of consciousness on what happens in them, around them, and to them.

Centering Prayer, when it reaches full consent to our nothingness, and when the closeness of God becomes a permanent experience, is the perfect preparation for death, because it is death—one has already died to the false self in the Night of Sense and has died to the ego in the Night of Spirit—and so is there any self left at all? Even the True Self has been transcended.

The dying person may advance in varying degrees into these levels which are the full fruits of Centering Prayer. But those who have practiced Centering Prayer have the greatest likelihood of manifesting in their own dying process some of these examples. It's not predictable, however, because it's a unique experience. Some saints have died in an ecstasy of love, and others, like Jesus, in an agony of torment. It depends what mystery they are called to, not just to channel but to enable Christ to relive in them. So Christ is dying in them, "precious in the eyes of God is the death of his saints" because they are manifesting in their particular humanity, in the degree that God wants, and for his purposes, the actual redeeming life of Christ that has been transmitted to them and through which they now, through their own sufferings, can transmit to others. Death, then, is not the end of anything, but the final completion of this process and the triumph of the grace of God.

FR. CARL: Thomas, do you see these remaining years of your life as preparing to come home?

FR. THOMAS: Well, I hope I am home! It's true I'm always stumbling around, but I made my decision–a desperate decision—to come home to God when I was 17 or 18. Not that I've come home as much as I would like to–but it's a journey that never ends, because what is home? It is "to live in the house of the Lord all the days of our lives." And that house is our participation in the divine life through grace. I presume there can always become more at-homeness.

FR. CARL: So it's living in the present moment. You're at home.

FR. THOMAS: Yes. Where else is there to go? I have difficulty remembering the past–What's the point? Whatever good is in the past is present in each of us right now, and this is what God sees. Theological hope is rooted in the infinite mercy and power of God, a combination that is sure-fire, you might say, because it does not rely on one's self or one's good deeds, or some huge mass of merit from a particular event in one's past life.

It's not about those partial responses to God, which are stepping stones towards communion. We are talking about a communion and a unity that is incomparable, that is genuine oneness.

Every now and then there's some delightful insight into that oneness, but it does not last long, or you would die, because it would be unbearable to return to the dusts of this world. We need to be patient between going too soon and arriving at the eternal banquet of love a little ahead of schedule. The authorities wouldn't know what to do with us! Do not delay it unduly either when you are being called because the right time to go has been figured out exactly. It will not be delayed by a single second, and it will not be anticipated by a single second.

If we really trust God, we don't have a care in the world. God takes care of everything. So being more or less there, as much as you can, is the project for the end of life. Being there is accelerated and brought to completion in the dying process and with death itself. Wasn't it Bach who has a chorale called "Come Sweet Death?" Well, it is sweet when it is perceived as the last barrier to total immersion in God or loss of self. Death in God is the fullness of life in this spaciousness that is the home of everything that is.

EPILOGUE

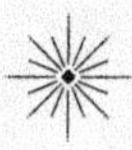

What I would like to leave behind is a simple prayer
that each of you may find what I have found—
God's special gift to us all: the gift of peace. When we
are at peace, we fnd the freedom to be most fully who
we are, even in the worst of times. We let go of what is
non-essential and embrace what is essential. We empty
ourselves so that God may more fully work within us.
And we become instruments in the hands of the Lord.

—JOSEPH CARDINAL BERNARDIN, *The Gift of Peace*

May the Lord bless you all the days of your life.

—PSALM 128: 5

Amen

FATHER THOMAS KEATING (1923–2018)

Father Thomas Keating was a Trappist monk, priest, and one of the principal architects of the Centering Prayer movement, which revitalized the Christian contemplative tradition for contemporary seekers. Born in New York City in 1923, Keating pursued studies at Yale University and Fordham University before entering the Cistercian Order in 1944. He was ordained a priest in 1949.

In the 1970s, while serving as abbot of St. Joseph's Abbey in Spencer, Massachusetts, Keating, alongside fellow monks Fathers William Meninger and Basil Pennington, developed Centering Prayer—a method inspired by the 14th-century spiritual classic *The Cloud of Unknowing*. This practice emphasizes silent, wordless prayer as a means of consenting to God's presence and action within.

To support and disseminate this contemplative practice, Keating co-founded Contemplative Outreach in 1984, an international organization dedicated to teaching Centering Prayer and fostering spiritual growth. A prolific author, Keating's works include *Open Mind, Open Heart, Invitation to Love,* and *The Human Condition,* among others. His teachings continue to guide individuals seeking a deeper relationship with the Divine through the path of contemplative silence.

At Wayfarer Books we believe poetry is the language of the earth. We believe words, like rivers through wild places, can change the shape of the world. We publish poets and writers and renegades who stand outside of mainstream culture; poets, essayists, and storytellers whose work might withstand the scrutiny of crows and coyotes, those who are cryptic and floral, the crepuscular, and the queer-at-heart. We are more than just a publisher but a community of writers. Our mission is to produce books that can serve as a compass and map to all wayfarers through wild terrain.

WAYFARERBOOKS.ORG

www.ingramcontent.com/pod-product-compliance
Lightning Source LLC
Chambersburg PA
CBHW051002050726
47592CB00007B/2670